PIANO SOLO

THE BEST CLASSICAL MUSIC EVER

ISBN 0-634-02121-4

HAL•LEONARD®
CORPORATION

7777 W. BLUEMOUND RD. P.O. BOX 13819 MILWAUKEE, WI 53213

Visit Hal Leonard Online at
www.halleonard.com

THE BEST CLASSI

CAL MUSIC EVER

Adagio in G Minor

Tomaso Albinoni
1671–1751
originally for organ and strings

Jesu, Joy of Man's Desiring

Jesus bleibet meine Freude

from Cantata No. 147, HERZ UND MUND UND TAT UND LEBEN

Johann Sebastian Bach
1685–1750
BWV 147
originally for choir and orchestra

Moderato

Air on the G String

from the Orchestral Suite No. 3 in D

Johann Sebastian Bach
1685–1750
BWV 1068
originally for orchestra

Prelude in C Major
from THE WELL-TEMPERED CLAVIER, BOOK 1

Johann Sebastian Bach
1685–1750

[Allegro]

Symphony No. 9
Fourth Movement Excerpt
("Ode to Joy")

Ludwig van Beethoven
1770–1827
Op. 125
originally for chorus and orchestra

original key: D Major

Für Elise

(For Elise)

Ludwig van Beethoven
1770–1827
WoO 59

Poco moto

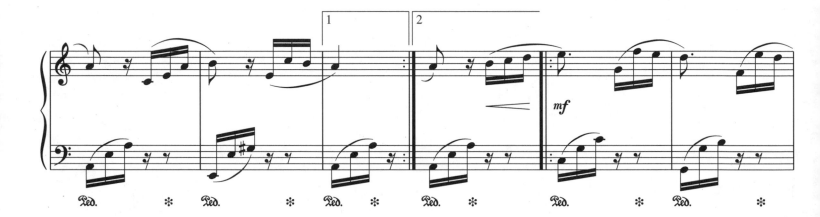

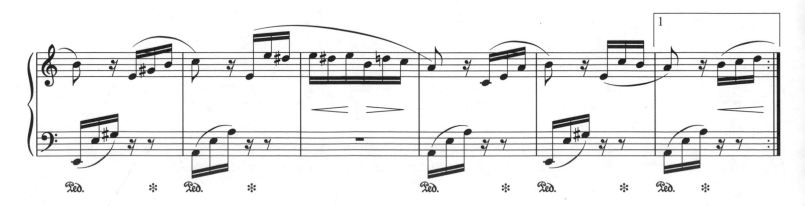

Symphony No. 3

"Eroica"
First Movement Excerpt

Ludwig van Beethoven
1770–1827
Op. 55
originally for orchestra

Allegro con brio

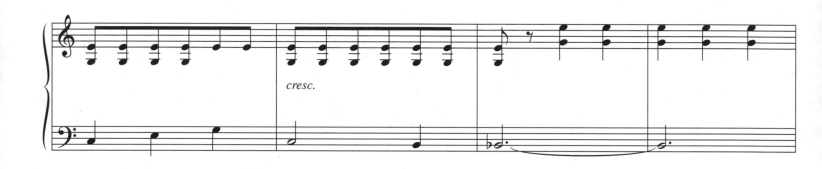

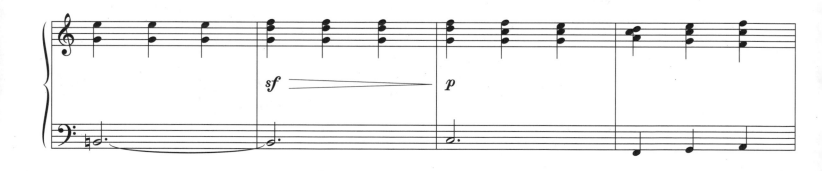

original key: E-flat Major

32

Symphony No. 5

First Movement Excerpt

Ludwig van Beethoven
1770–1827
Op. 67
originally for orchestra

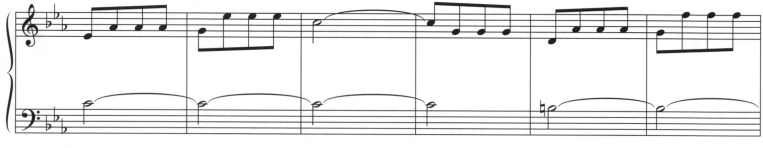

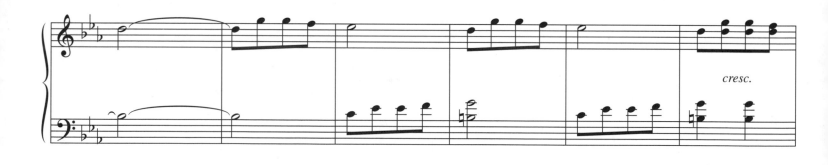

Turkish March
from THE RUINS OF ATHENS

Ludwig van Beethoven
1770–1827
Op. 113
originally for orchestra

Toreador Song

from the opera CARMEN

Georges Bizet
1838–1875

Allegro moderato

Habanera
from the opera CARMEN

Georges Bizet
1838–1875

Symphony No. 1
Fourth Movement Excerpt

Johannes Brahms
1830–1897
Op. 68
originally for orchestra

Allegro non troppo ma con brio

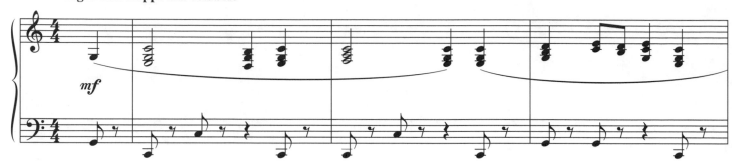

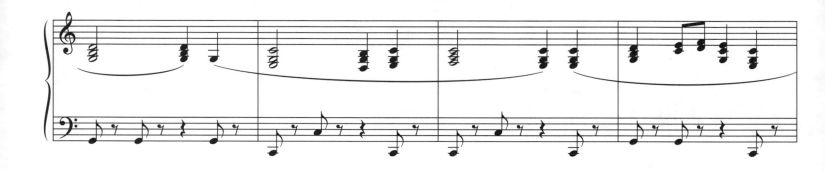

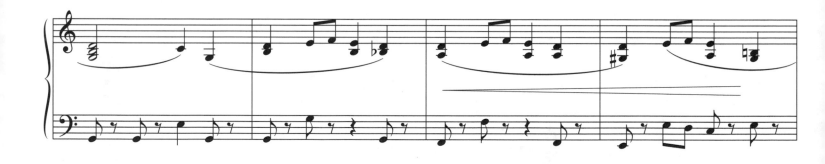

Symphony No. 4
First Movement Excerpt

Johannes Brahms
1830–1897
Op. 98
originally for orchestra

Allegro non troppo

Lullaby
(Wiegenlied)

Johannes Brahms
1830–1897
Op. 49, No. 4
originally for voice and piano

Dolce, con moto

Mazurka in E Minor

Fryderyk Chopin
1810–1849
Op. 17, No. 2

Lento, ma non troppo ♩ = 144

Prelude in A Major

Fryderyk Chopin
1810–1849
Op. 28, No. 7

Prelude in C Minor

Fryderyk Chopin
1810–1849
Op. 28, No. 20

Prelude in B Minor

Fryderyk Chopin
1810–1849
Op. 28, No. 6

Lento assai

Prelude in E Minor

Fryderyk Chopin
1810–1849
Op. 28, No. 4

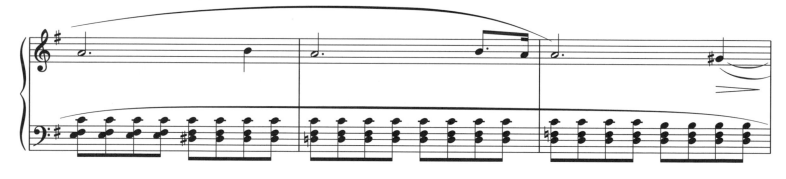

Waltz in D-flat Major
("Minute Waltz")

Fryderyk Chopin
1810–1849
Op. 64, No. 1

The Girl with the Flaxen Hair
(La fille aux cheveux de lin)

Claude Debussy
1862–1918

Rêverie

Claude Debussy
1862–1918

Andante sans lenteur (not too slowly)

pp *très doux et très expressif*
(gently, expressively)

Pizzicato Polka
from the ballet SYLVIA

Léo Delibes
1836–1891
originally for orchestra

Una furtiva lagrima

from the opera L'ELISIR D'AMORE
(The Elixir of Love)

Gaetano Donizetti
1797–1848

Symphony No. 9

"From the New World"
Second Movement Excerpt

Antonín Dvořák
1841–1904
Op. 95
originally for orchestra

Slavonic Dance

Excerpt

Antonín Dvořák
1841–1904
Op. 46, No. 1
originally for piano, four hands
orchestrated by the composer

Spinning Song
(Spinnliedchen)

Albert Ellmenreich
1816–1905
Op. 14, No. 4

Allegretto

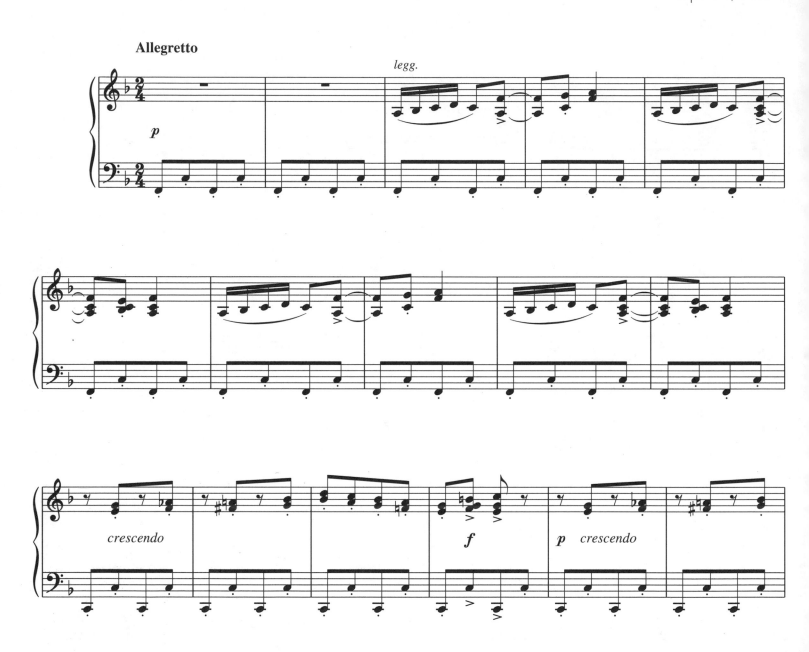

Pavane
Excerpt

Gabriel Fauré
1845–1924
Op. 50
originally for chorus and orchestra

Andante molto moderato

original key: F-sharp Minor

Après un rêve
(After a Dream)

Gabriel Fauré
1845–1924
Op. 7, No. 1
originally for voice and piano

Panis angelicus

César Franck
1822–1890
originally for tenor and
instrumental ensemble

Ave Maria

based on Prelude in C Major by J.S. Bach

Charles Gounod
1818–1893
originally for chamber ensemble

Andante con moto

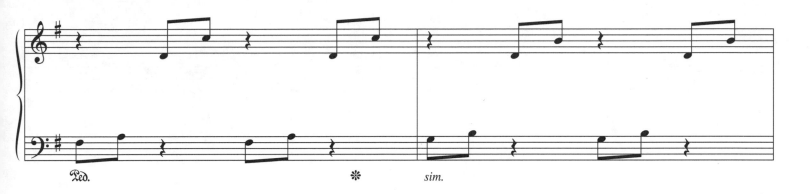

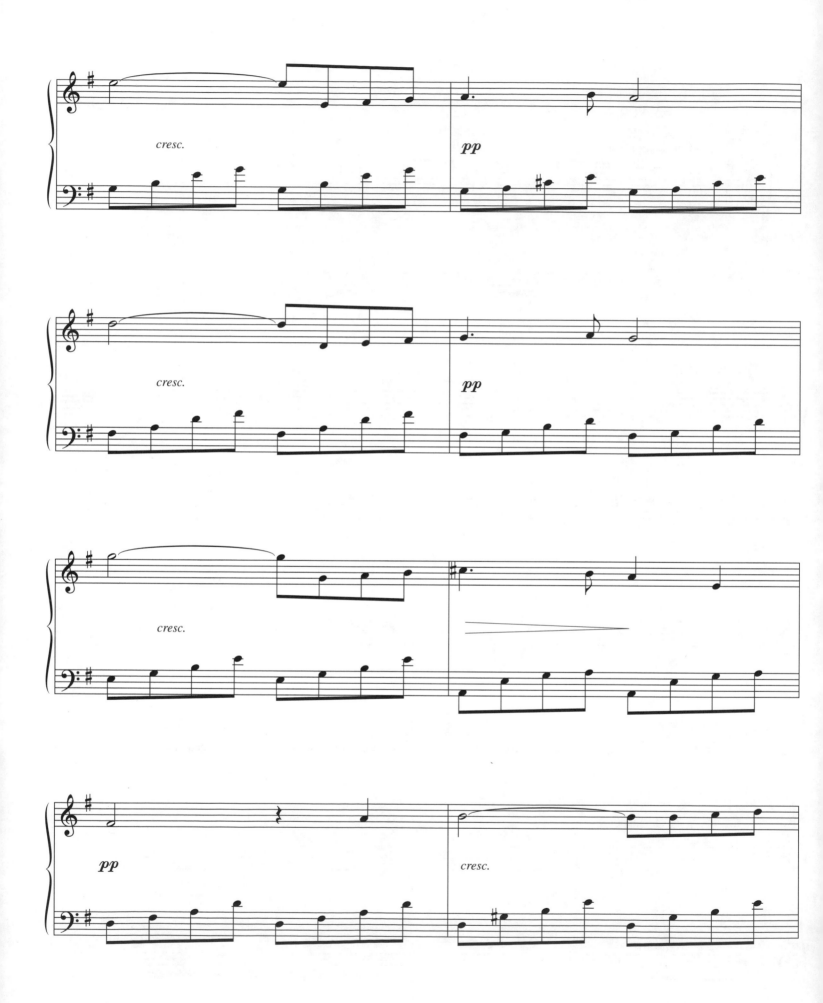

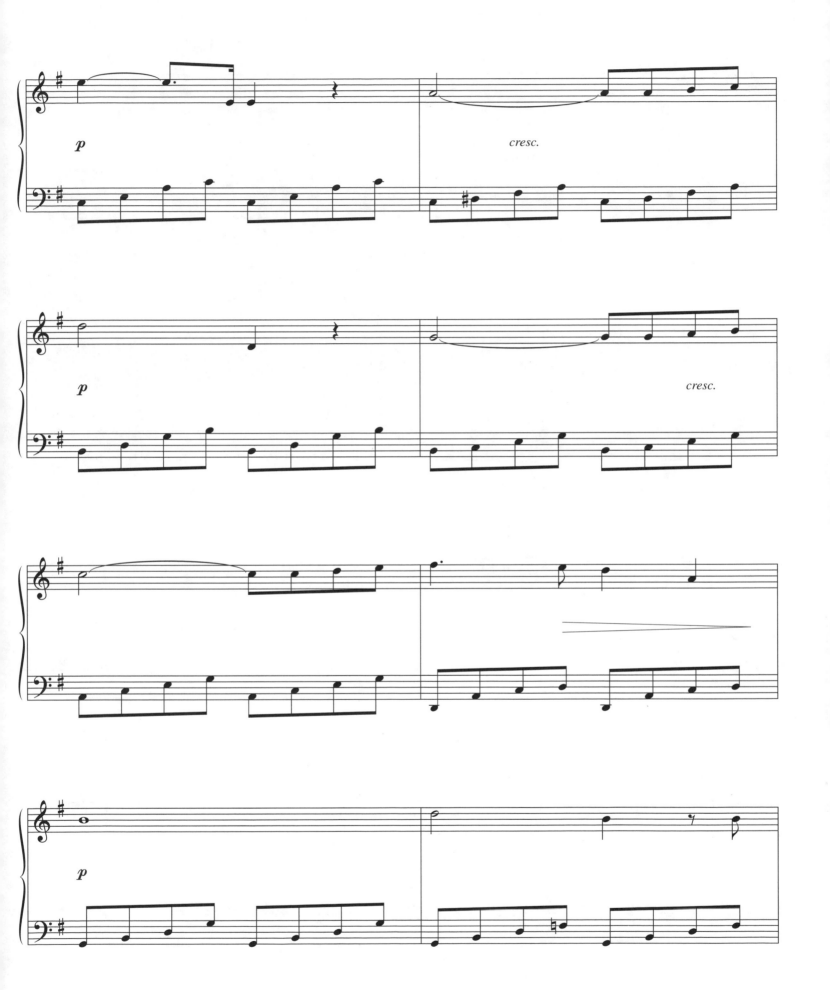

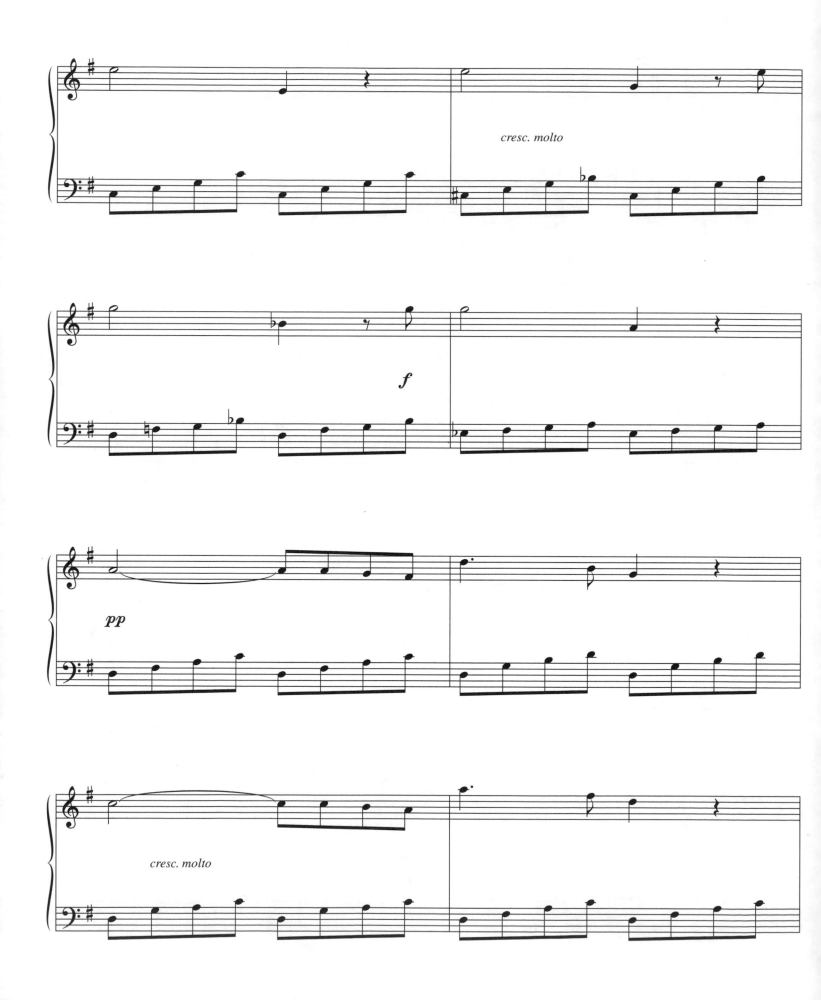

Funeral March of a Marionette
Themes

Charles Gounod
1818–1893
originally for orchestra

In the Hall of the Mountain King

from PEER GYNT

Edvard Grieg
1843–1907
Op. 23, No. 7
originally for orchestra

Alla marcia e molto marcato

Morning

from PEER GYNT

Edvard Grieg
1843–1907
Op. 23, No. 13
originally for orchestra

original key: E Major

Allegro maestoso

from WATER MUSIC

Excerpt

George Frideric Handel
1685–1759
originally for orchestra

Allegro maestoso

original key: D Major

I Know That My Redeemer Liveth

from the oratorio MESSIAH
Excerpt

George Frideric Handel
1685–1759
originally for orchestra

Hallelujah

from the oratorio MESSIAH
Excerpt

George Frideric Handel
1685–1759
originally for chorus and orchestra

Allegretto moderato

Largo

"Ombra mai fù"
from the opera SERSE
(Xerxes)

George Frideric Handel
1685–1759

Pastoral Symphony
from the oratorio MESSIAH

George Frideric Handel
1685–1759
originally for orchestra

Trumpet Concerto in E-flat Major

First Movement Excerpt

Franz Joseph Haydn
1732–1809
originally for trumpet and orchestra

Symphony No. 2
"Resurrection"
Fifth Movement Choral Theme

Gustav Mahler
1860–1911
originally for soloists,
chorus and orchestra

original key: G-flat Major

Evening Prayer
from the opera HANSEL AND GRETEL

Engelbert Humperdinck
1854–1921

Vesti, la giubba

from the opera I PAGLIACCI

(The Clowns)

Ruggero Leoncavallo
1857–1919

To a Wild Rose
from WOODLAND SKETCHES

Edward MacDowell
1860–1908
Op. 51

With simple tenderness ♩ = 88

slightly marked

Meditation
from the opera THAÏS

Jules Massenet
1842–1912

A Midsummer Night's Dream

Overture Themes

Felix Mendelssohn
1809–1847
Op. 61
originally for orchestra

Allegro di molto

original key: E Major

"Fingal's Cave" Overture

or "The Hebrides"
Themes

Felix Mendelssohn
1809–1847
Op. 26
originally for orchestra

Allegro moderato

Symphony No. 4

"Italian"
First Movement Excerpt

Felix Mendelssohn
1809–1847
Op. 90
originally for orchestra

Allegro vivace

original key: A Major

Eine kleine Nachtmusik

(A Little Night Music)
First Movement Excerpt

Wolfgang Amadeus Mozart
1756–1791
K 525
originally for string ensemble

157

Ave verum corpus

Wolfgang Amadeus Mozart
1756–1791
K 618
originally for chorus and orchestra

Là ci darem la mano
from the opera DON GIOVANNI

Wolfgang Amadeus Mozart
1756–1791

Lacrymosa
from REQUIEM

Wolfgang Amadeus Mozart
1756–1791
K 626
originally for chorus and orchestra

Larghetto

Papageno's Song
from the opera THE MAGIC FLUTE

Wolfgang Amadeus Mozart
1756–1791

Piano Concerto No. 21

"Elvira Madigan"
Second Movement Excerpt

Wolfgang Amadeus Mozart
1756–1791
K 467
originally for piano and orchestra

Symphony No. 40
First Movement Excerpt

Wolfgang Amadeus Mozart
1756–1791
K 550
originally for orchestra

original key: G Minor

Queen of the Night's Vengeance Aria
from the opera THE MAGIC FLUTE

Wolfgang Amadeus Mozart
1756–1791

Allegro assai

Symphony No. 41

"Jupiter"
First Movement Excerpt

Wolfgang Amadeus Mozart
1756–1791
K 551
originally for orchestra

Allegro vivace

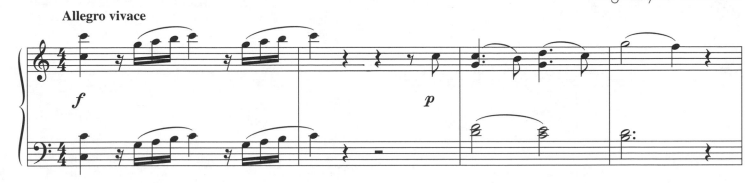

Rondeau

Excerpt

Jean Joseph Mouret
1682–1738
originally for orchestra

Canon
Excerpt

Johann Pachelbel
1653–1706
originally for 3 violins and continuo

Adagio

original key: D Major

Can Can

from the opera ORPHEUS IN THE UNDERWORLD

Jacques Offenbach
1819–1880
originally for chorus and orchestra

Barcarolle
from the opera THE TALES OF HOFFMANN

Jacques Offenbach
1819–1880
originally for singers, chorus and orchestra

Moderato

pp

molto cantabile

original key: D Major

Vissi d'arte
from the opera TOSCA

Giacomo Puccini
1858–1924

Andante lento appassionato

O mio babbino caro

from the opera GIANNI SCHICCHI

Giacomo Puccini
1858–1924

Andante ingenuo

O soave fanciulla

from the opera LA BOHÈME
(The Bohemian Life)

Giacomo Puccini
1858–1924

Largo sostenuto ($\bullet$ = 58)

Quando men vo
(Musetta's Waltz)
from the opera LA BOHÈME
(The Bohemian Life)

Giacomo Puccini
1858–1924

Un bel dì vedremo

from the opera MADAMA BUTTERFLY

Giacomo Puccini
1858–1924

Sostendo molto

Sheherazade
Themes from Part 1

Nikolay Rimsky-Korsakov
1844–1908
Op. 35
originally for orchestra

William Tell Overture

from the opera GUILLAUME TELL
(William Tell)

Gioacchino Rossini
1792–1868
originally for orchestra

original key: E Major

The Swan
from CARNIVAL OF THE ANIMALS

Camille Saint-Saëns
1835–1921
originally for chamber ensemble

Gymnopédie No. 1

Erik Satie
1866–1925

Lent et douloureux (slowly and mournfully)

Ave Maria

Franz Schubert
1797–1828
D. 839
originally for voice and piano

Symphony No. 8

"Unfinished"
First Movement Excerpt

Franz Schubert
1797–1828
D. 759
originally for orchestra

Allegro moderato

original key: B Minor

The Happy Farmer Returning from Work

(Fröhlicher Landmann, von der Arbeit zurückkehrend)

from ALBUM FÜR DIE JUGEND

(Album for the Young)

Robert Schumann
1810–1856
Op. 68, No. 10

By the Beautiful Blue Danube

Themes

Johann Strauss, Jr.
1825–1899
Op. 317
originally for orchestra

Tempo di Valse

Emperor Waltz

Excerpt

Johann Strauss, Jr.
1825–1899
Op. 437
originally for orchestra

Slow March Tempo

Tales from the Vienna Woods

Themes

Johann Strauss, Jr.
1825–1899
Op. 325
originally for orchestra

Tempo di Valse

Dance of the Sugar Plum Fairy

from the ballet THE NUTCRACKER

Pyotr Il'yich Tchaikovsky
1840–1893
Op. 71
originally for orchestra

Andante ma non troppo

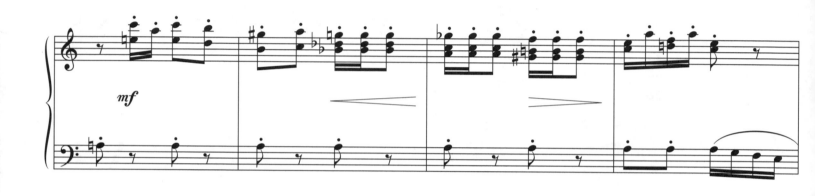

1812 Overture

Excerpt

Pyotr Il'yich Tchaikovsky
1840–1893
Op. 49
originally for orchestra

Piano Concerto No. 1
First Movement Excerpt

Pyotr Il'yich Tchaikovsky
1840–1893
Op. 23
originally for piano and orchestra

Andante maestoso

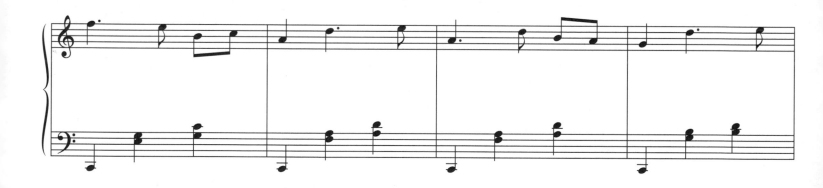

original key: B-flat Minor

dim. e rall.

8vb

ROMEO AND JULIET
"Love Theme"
Excerpt

Pyotr Il'yich Tchaikovsky
1840–1893
originally for orchestra

Allegro giusto, con espressione

mf legato e dolce

original key: D-flat Major

Waltz of the Flowers
from the ballet THE NUTCRACKER
Excerpt

Pyotr Il'yich Tchaikovsky
1840–1893
Op. 71
originally for orchestra

original key: D Major

Libiamo
from the opera LA TRAVIATA
(The Fallen Woman)

Giuseppe Verdi
1813–1901

La donna è mobile

from the opera RIGOLETTO

Giuseppe Verdi
1813–1901

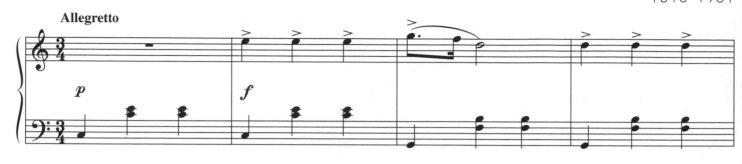

Triumphal March
from the opera AÏDA

Giuseppe Verdi
1813–1901

Allegro moderato

Mandolin Concerto in C Major
First Movement Excerpt

Antonio Vivaldi
1678–1741
originally for mandolin and orchestra

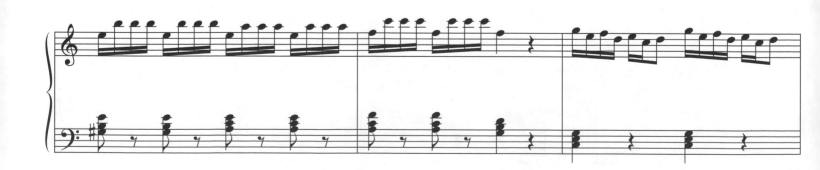

Pilgrims' Chorus
from the opera TANNHÄUSER

Richard Wagner
1813–1883

Andante maestoso

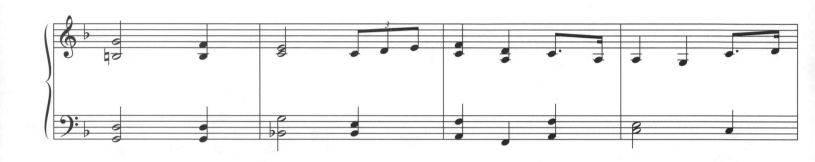

The Greatest Songs Ever Written

The Best Ever Collection
Arranged for Piano, Voice & Guitar

150 of the Most Beautiful Songs Ever
Over 400 pages of slow and sentimental ballads, including: Edelweiss • For All We Know • How Deep Is Your Love • I Have Dreamed • I'll Be Seeing You • If We Only Have Love • Songbird • Summertime • Unchained Melody • Young at Heart • many more.
00360735...$19.95

The Best Big Band Songs Ever
69 of the greatest big band songs ever, including: Basin Street Blues • Boogie Woogie Bugle Boy • Don't Get Around Much Anymore • In the Mood • Marie • Moonglow • Opus One • Satin Doll • Sentimental Journey • String of Pearls • Who's Sorry Now.
00359129...$16.95

The Best Broadway Songs Ever
Over 65 songs in all! Highlights include: All I Ask of You • Bess, You Is My Woman • Camelot • Climb Ev'ry Mountain • Comedy Tonight • Don't Cry for Me Argentina • Getting to Know You • I Dreamed a Dream • If I Were a Rich Man • Ol' Man River • and more!
00309155...$19.95

The Best Christmas Songs Ever
A collection of 72 of the most-loved songs of the season, including: Frosty the Snow Man • A Holly Jolly Christmas • Home for the Holidays • I'll Be Home for Christmas • Jingle-Bell Rock • Rudolph, The Red-Nosed Reindeer • Silver Bells • Toyland • more.
00359130 ....$18.95

The Best Classical Songs Ever
Over 80 of the best songs in classical music, including: Air on the G String • Ave Maria • Canon in D • Eine Kleine Nachtmusik • Für Elise • Lacrymosa • Ode to Joy • William Tell Overture • and many more.
00310674...$17.95

The Best Contemporary Christian Songs Ever
A great collection of 50 favorites by top artists. Includes: Awesome God • El Shaddai • Father's Eyes • Friends • God Is in Control • In the Name of the Lord • Jesus Freak • People Need the Lord • Place in This World • Serve the Lord • Thank You • Thy Word • more.
00310558...$19.95

The Best Country Songs Ever
Over 65 songs, featuring: Always on My Mind • Crazy • Daddy Sang Bass • Forever and Ever, Amen • God Bless the U.S.A. • I Fall to Pieces • Stand By Your Man • Through the Years • and more.
00359135...$16.95

The Best Easy Listening Songs Ever
A collection of 75 mellow favorites, featuring: All Out of Love • (They Long to Be) Close to You • Every Breath You Take • Eye in the Sky • How Am I Supposed to Live Without You • Imagine • Love Takes Time • Unchained Melody • Vision of Love • Your Song.
00359193...$18.95

The Best Gospel Songs Ever
80 of the best-loved gospel songs of all time: Amazing Grace • Daddy Sang Bass • His Eye Is on the Sparrow • How Great Thou Art • I'll Fly Away • Just a Closer Walk with Thee • Just a Little Talk with Jesus • The Old Rugged Cross • Will the Circle Be Unbroken • more.
00310503...$19.95

The Best Jazz Standards Ever
77 of the greatest jazz hits of all time, including: April in Paris • Body and Soul • Don't Get Around Much Anymore • Love Is Here to Stay • Misty • Out of Nowhere • Satin Doll • Unforgettable • When I Fall in Love • and many more.
00311641...$17.95

The Best Latin Songs Ever
67 songs, including: Adios • Besame Mucho (Kiss Me Much) • Blame It on the Bossa Nova • The Girl from Ipanema • Green Eyes • How Insensitive (Insensatez) • Malaguena • One Not Samba • Slightly Out of Tune (Desafinado) • Summer Samba (So Nice) • and more.
00310355...$17.95

The Best Love Songs Ever
A collection of 66 favorite love songs, including: (They Long to Be) Close to You • Endless Love • Here and Now • Longer • Love Takes Time • Misty • My Funny Valentine • So in Love • You Needed Me • Your Song.
00359198...$17.95

The Best Movie Songs Ever – 2nd Edition
This newly revised edition includes 74 songs made famous on the silver screen: Almost Paradise • Chariots of Fire • Circle of Life • I Will Wait for You • My Heart Will Go On • Take My Breath Away • Unchained Melody • You'll Be in My Heart • more.
00310063...$19.95

The Best R&B Songs Ever
66 songs, including: After the Love Has Gone • Baby Love • Dancing in the Street • Endless Love • Here and Now • I Will Survive • Saving All My Love for You • Stand By Me • What's Going On • and more.
00310184...$19.95

The Best Rock Songs Ever
70 songs, including: All Shook Up • Ballroom Blitz • Bennie and The Jets • Blue Suede Shoes • Born to Be Wild • Boys Are Back in Town • Every Breath You Take • Faith • Free Bird • Hey Jude • Louie, Louie • Maggie May • Money • We Got the Beat • Wild Thing • more!
00490424...$17.95

The Best Songs Ever
Over 70 must-own classics, including: All I Ask of You • Body and Soul • Crazy • Edelweiss • Love Me Tender • Memory • Moonlight in Vermont • My Funny Valentine • People • Satin Doll • Save the Best for Last • Strangers in the Night • Tears in Heaven • Unforgettable • The Way We Were • A Whole New World • and more.
00359224...$19.95

More of the Best Songs Ever
79 more favorites, including: Alfie • April in Paris • Autumn in New York • Beauty and the Beast • Beyond the Sea • Candle in the Wind • Don't Get Around Much Anymore • Endless Love • Falling in Love with Love • The First Time Ever I Saw Your Face • I've Got the World on a String • I've Grown Accustomed to Her Face • Misty • My Blue Heaven • My Heart Will Go On • Stella by Starlight • Witchcraft • more.
00310437...$19.95

The Best Standards Ever
Volume 1 (A-L)
72 beautiful ballads, including: All the Things You Are • Bewitched • Getting to Know You • God Bless' the Child • Hello, Young Lovers • It's Only a Paper Moon • I've Got You Under My Skin • The Lady Is a Tramp • Little White Lies.
00359231...$15.95

Volume 2 (M-Z)
72 songs, including: Makin' Whoopee • Misty • Moonlight in Vermont • My Funny Valentine • Old Devil Moon • The Party's Over • People Will Say We're in Love • Smoke Gets in Your Eyes • Strangers in the Night • Tuxedo Junction • Yesterday.
00359232...$15.95

FOR MORE INFORMATION, SEE YOUR LOCAL MUSIC DEALER
OR WRITE TO:

HAL•LEONARD
CORPORATION
7777 W. BLUEMOUND RD. P.O. BOX 13819 MILWAUKEE, WI 5321

www.halleonard.com

Prices, contents and availability subject to change without notice. Not all products available outside the U.S.A.

0800